Ivanka Trump

Ivanka Trump

A Brand of Her Own

MATT DOEDEN

LERNER PUBLICATIONS ◆ MINNEAPOLIS

Lerner Publications Company
A division of Lerner Publishing Group, Inc.
241 First Avenue North
Minneapolis, MN USA 55401

For reading levels and more information, look up this title at www.lernerbooks.com.

The images in this book are used with the permission of: © Jeff Swensen/Getty Images, p. 2; Mark Reinstein/ZUMA Press/Newscom, p. 6; AP Photo/John Locher, p. 8; REUTERS/Alamy Stock Photo, p. 10; © Davidoff Studios/Getty Images, p. 11; AP Photo/Remy de la Mauviniere, p. 12; AP Photo/Kathy Willens, p. 13; © Daderot/Wikimedia Commons (PD), p. 14; AP Photo/Diane Bondareff, p. 15; © Stephane Cardinale/Sygma/Getty Images, p. 17; Klaus Nowottnick/picture-alliance/dpa/AP Images, p. 18; © Jon Kopaloff/FilmMagic/Getty Images, p. 19; Vespasian/Alamy Stock Photo, p. 20; AP Photo/Sipa USA, pp. 21, 34; Arcaid Images/Alamy Stock Photo, p. 23; Francis Specker/Alamy Stock Photo, p. 25; © Frederick M. Brown/Getty Images, p. 26; Everett Collection Inc/Alamy Stock Photo, p. 27; WENN Ltd/Alamy Stock Photo, p. 28; ZUMA Press, Inc./Alamy Stock Photo, p. 29; © Brian Marcus/Fred Marcus Photography/Getty Images, p. 30; AP Photo/John Minchillo, p. 31; © Michele Eve Sandberg/Corbis/Getty Images, p. 32; © Laura Cavanaugh/FilmMagic/Getty Images, p. 36; AP Photo/Evan Vucci, p. 37; © MANDEL NGAN/AFP/Getty Images, p. 38; © Mark Makela/Getty Images, p. 39; © Mark Wilson/Getty Images, p. 40.

Front Cover: REUTERS/Rick Wilking/Newscom.

Main body text set in Rotis Serif Std 55 Regular 13.5/17. Typeface provided by Adobe Systems.

Library of Congress Cataloging-in-Publication Data

The Cataloging-in-Publication Data for *Ivanka Trump: A Brand of Her Own* is on file at the Library of Congress.
ISBN 978-1-5124-8624-7 (lib. bdg.)
ISBN 978-1-5124-8625-4 (EB pdf)

Manufactured in the United States of America
1-43426-33196-3/28/2017

JB
Tru

CONTENTS

Ivanka Trump speaks in support of her father's candidacy for president at the 2016 Republican National Convention.

The crowd at the Quicken Loans Arena in Cleveland, Ohio, roared as thirty-four-year-old Ivanka Trump stepped to the podium to the tune of the Beatles' "Here Comes the Sun." It was the final night of the 2016 Republican National Convention. Trump was coming out to introduce her father, Donald Trump, as the presidential nominee of the Republican Party.

"We love you, Ivanka!" shouted a man in the crowd as she prepared to speak. The remark echoed the thoughts of many in the arena that night. While Donald Trump remained a controversial figure even within his own political party, his daughter seemed almost universally liked. It was a main reason she'd been chosen for this spotlight. Her calm manner and careful way with words made her a perfect counterpart to her father, who had a tendency to say whatever came to mind. She would be the last to speak before her father accepted the nomination. The eyes of the United States and the rest of the world were on her.

Trump appeared confident as she stood on the podium. Her self-assured smile didn't tell the whole story, though. She knew how big this stage was, and she later admitted that she was terrified. Often, when a member of a candidate's family speaks at such an event, their words are largely directed by the campaign staff. That wasn't the case for Trump. She was on her own. "[My dad has] totally left [what to say] up to me," she said in an interview in the days leading up to the event. "I wish he'd give me input. But you know, I think he wants it to come from my heart."

Ivanka Trump was met with cheers and applause from the Republican National Convention crowd.

Trump let little of that nervousness show as the crowd quieted and she began her remarks. It would have been easy for her to echo previous speakers in praising her father's policies. She could have thrilled many there just by throwing out some easy catchphrases and campaign slogans. But Trump didn't do that. She understood that she wasn't just talking to the people in that arena. She was talking to voters all across the United States. One of the first things she said was that she didn't consider herself a Republican (or a Democrat). It was a bold statement, considering her audience.

Trump wasn't there to promote her father's policies. She made no mention of his campaign promises. Instead, her goal was to show Donald Trump as a real person and a father.

"I remember playing on the floor by my father's desk," she said, "constructing miniature buildings with Legos and Erector sets, while he did the same with concrete, steel, and glass. My father taught my siblings and me . . . that there's nothing that we cannot accomplish, if we marry vision and passion with an enduring work ethic."

She went on to detail some of the issues close to her, including equal pay for women and affordable childcare. They were the sort of issues rarely discussed at a Republican National Convention, yet she managed to raise them in a way that most in attendance embraced.

She said, "This is the fighter, the doer, that you have chosen as your nominee. . . . I've loved and respected him my entire life. And I could not be more proud tonight to present to you, and to all of America, my father and our next president, Donald J. Trump."

Donald Trump followed with a seventy-five-minute acceptance speech. Yet for many, it was Ivanka Trump's time onstage that stole the show. California delegate Shawn Steel called her speech "the high point of the convention for me. . . ." He added, "This woman, I've been saying for some time, is the greatest asset Donald Trump has."

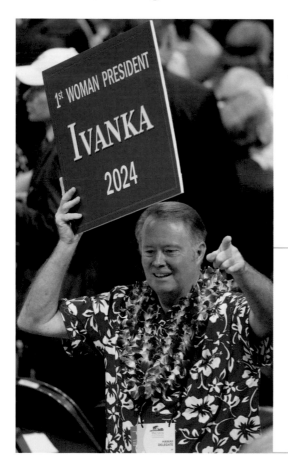

That feeling was shared by most in attendance. Yet some took their support a step further. One sign in the crowd read: "Ivanka 2024. First Female President."

Signs printed with various slogans promoting Ivanka Trump as future US president were popular on the night she introduced her father as the 2016 Republican presidential nominee.

Childhood on Display

Ivanka Maria Trump was born on October 30, 1981, in Manhattan, New York. The second child of Donald and Ivana Trump, she was born into a family of wealth and privilege. Donald Trump was a successful real estate developer. Ivana had once worked as a fashion model.

Ivanka grew up alongside older brother, Donald Jr., and younger brother Eric in the heart of Manhattan. They lived in a lavish home on the sixty-eighth floor of Trump Tower. Her parents' wealth and relative fame made them major players in the Manhattan social scene.

A young Ivanka poses for a photo with her parents and brother Eric.

Ivana Trump strides down the runway in a jacket and a gold dress in her days as a fashion model.

Her parents were different in many ways. Ivanka Trump credits both in forming aspects of her personality. Her mother was born and grew up in the European nation of Czechoslovakia (now the Czech Republic). She passed on her sense of worldliness and culture to her daughter. Donald Trump, meanwhile, passed on his driven and competitive nature.

From an early age, there was little doubt among the family members that Ivanka was a daddy's girl. Father and daughter shared an extremely tight bond. Since Donald Trump was frequently away on business, little Ivanka took every chance to spend time with him at home—even if he was busy working.

"I'd sit on the floor [of his office] and hear him bid out contracts," Ivanka recalled. "I just liked it."

Celebrity and wealth had their benefits. But they also came with some serious drawbacks. That became clear to Ivanka when scandal rocked the family in 1989.

Donald Trump was caught having an affair with a woman named Marla Maples. Reporters hounded the family. Photographers lurked outside the family's home, hoping to snap candid photos of the Trumps. They even showed up outside Ivanka's school.

Ivanka's world was crumbling around her, and the ordeal was on display for the world to see. She was miserable. During this time, Ivanka developed a strong distrust of the press, a feeling that she would carry into adulthood. Yet she also believes that enduring the media's scrutiny made her stronger.

"[The experience] gave me a glimpse into how ugly the world can be," Ivanka later explained. "And I think it made me a little bit more resilient."

The marriage did not survive the scandal. Donald and Ivana Trump divorced in 1991. He later married Maples, with whom he had a second daughter, Tiffany.

Donald Trump and Marla Maples at their wedding in 1993

Ivanka's life was further turned upside down when, at the age of fifteen, she transferred to Choate Rosemary Hall, a boarding school in Connecticut. Ivanka was not happy there. She was cut off from her friends back in

Choate Rosemary Hall in Wallingford, Connecticut, is one of the United States' most well-known college preparatory schools.

Manhattan. To her, the boarding school felt like a prison. She needed a way to escape and to assert her independence. It didn't take her long to figure out exactly how to do that.

Cover Girl

Ivanka's goals had always been to follow in the footsteps of her father and pursue a career in business. However, the fastest way for her to make her own mark was to take a different path—her mother's path. So the young teen, who had inherited her mother's high cheekbones and willowy frame, was ready to take on the world of modeling. After spending much of her life hiding from cameras, Ivanka was ready to step in front of them.

Ivanka Trump takes to the runway in New York at a Scottish-inspired fashion show called Dressed to Kilt.

Ivanka signed a modeling deal with Elite Model Management. It was a well-known and respected modeling agency. The agency's president, Monique Pillard, knew Donald Trump and had long thought Ivanka would be well suited for a modeling career.

Not everyone in the modeling industry was convinced that Ivanka belonged, however. Critics said that Elite had hired her because of her name more than her look. Audrey Roatta, a senior assistant to Pillard, quickly dismissed such talk. "She would be a model [without the Trump name], and she would be with Elite," Roatta insisted. "She understands that of course her name helped in the beginning to get her foot in the door. She's not stupid. But she also knows that she will be treated like any other model when it comes to clients."

Ivana Trump, who had spent time in the competitive world of high fashion, wasn't convinced that letting her daughter model was such a good idea. She wanted Ivanka to focus on her studies, not on the runway. Ivana Trump insisted that Ivanka model only on weekends and holidays. When school was in session, Ivanka was to give her studies her full attention.

Whether it was her name or her looks—or a bit of both—Ivanka's career quickly took off. Soon she was strutting up and down runways. She modeled for major designers, including Versace, Marc Bouwer, and Thierry Mugler.

Ivanka Trump dons a red high-collared top and red eye makeup to match on the catwalk.

Ivanka's big opportunity in modeling came when she landed the cover for the May 1997 issue of *Seventeen* magazine. On the cover, she wore an airy blue floral-print sleeveless dress over a simple white camisole. Inside, the magazine featured a photo spread of Ivanka in her dorm room at Choate. In an interview, Ivanka joked that at almost 5 feet 11 inches (1.8 meters) tall, she had to crouch just to see herself in the room's full-length mirror.

The opportunities kept coming. In August 1997, Ivanka made her television debut. She served as cohost for the 1997 Miss Teen USA pageant, which was owned by her father. "In my mind, there is no one more perfect for this," said Maureen Reidy, the president of the company that organized the pageant. "She is [a] 4.0 student, does a lot of [charity work], and is on her way to supermodel stardom."

It seemed as if Ivanka's future in modeling was bright. But the teenager had other plans. Modeling had never been a career choice for her. It had been a diversion and a good excuse to travel. It wasn't something she really enjoyed, and she had no plans to make a life out of it. Of more interest to her was a summer job her father gave her at the age of fifteen. She had to shadow, or follow, the foreman in the construction of the Trump World Tower in New York. Ivanka loved being on the job site. Actually building something was, to her, far more rewarding than modeling. And so, after a few short years, she turned away from the runway to focus exclusively on her studies. It was time to start preparing for the career she really wanted. It was time to start following in her father's footsteps.

New York City's Trump World Tower is one of the tallest and most expensive residential buildings in the world.

Business Minded

After graduating from Choate in 2000, Trump traveled to Washington, DC, to enroll at Georgetown University. While at Georgetown, she became involved with a documentary titled *Born Rich*. The documentary focused on children of very wealthy families. In it, director Jamie Johnson profiles Trump, along with other kids born into wealth.

The film was released to some critical acclaim in 2003. However, several of those featured in the film were upset with the final cut. They didn't like how Johnson portrayed them as petty and entitled. Most critics agree that Trump, however, stood out in contrast. According to Helen Pow of the *Daily Mail*, "Unlike others, the young real estate darling . . . came across [as] down-to-earth, never [disrespecting] her family or the privilege she was born into."

Ivanka Trump appears on camera with, *from left to right*: Condé Nast media company heir S. I. Newhouse IV; Josiah Hornblower, heir to the Vanderbilt/Whitney fortune; and Jamie Johnson, who directed *Born Rich*.

Trump spent two years at Georgetown. In 2002 she transferred to the Wharton School at the University of Pennsylvania. The business school had become something of a family legacy. Both her father and older brother had graduated from Wharton. Trump was determined to be the next in line.

Trump majored in finance and real estate, preparing for a future in the family business. She was a serious and dedicated student. In 2004 she graduated with honors.

The Wharton School is known for educating many of the United States' top entrepreneurs.

It would have been easy for Trump to jump directly into the family business. Joining her father's empire had always been her goal. But she had lived her whole life in her father's shadow. And while she understood that her name would open doors for her, she wanted to at least get a start on her own.

An Attractive Offer

In the spring of 2004, Trump was awakened by a phone call. She was on the verge of graduating, with just one final test remaining. After a night spent studying, she'd had only a few hours of sleep and considered letting the phone ring.

Instead, she picked it up. She was greeted by the voice of Anna Wintour, the editor of *Vogue* and a powerful voice in the world of fashion. Trump had always had a strong interest in fashion, and few things in the fashion world are bigger than *Vogue*. Wintour was one of Trump's personal heroes, and she was on the phone to offer the soon-to-be graduate a job.

It may have sounded like an offer that was too good to refuse. Yet that's exactly what Trump did. She'd already agreed to work for a real estate developer, and she wasn't going to go back on her word. So she turned Wintour down. Giving up a chance to work at *Vogue* left no doubt as to Trump's true career intentions.

Legendary fashion editor Anna Wintour is a hero to many in the fashion world.

So she accepted a job with Forest City Enterprises, a real estate developer run by Bruce Ratner. Her job was with the development team planning an upscale shopping mall called Ridge Hill in Yonkers, New York.

As her first day approached, Trump was obsessed with making a good first impression. Fearing she would show up late, she made a trial run to the site the day before she started. Trump took to New York's subway system and promptly got lost. Making matters worse, the trains weren't running on their normal weekday schedules because it was Labor Day. The entire trip was a disaster.

The next morning, with that memory fresh in her mind, Trump left nothing to chance. She set two alarms so she wouldn't oversleep. She left hours early to give herself time to get lost. This time, however, she knew which trains to take and they were all running on schedule. The commute took just twenty minutes, and Trump arrived at the office long before anyone else. The lights weren't even on yet! It was almost another two hours before anyone showed up to open the doors and let her inside.

The job was an entry-level position. It gave Trump a chance to get her hands dirty and deal with details. "She did everything," Ratner explained. Trump helped the team balance its finances, coordinated with mall tenants, and worked on the mall's future layout. "She was down-to-earth," Ratner said. "She worked like everybody else. There was no special privilege about her."

The high-end Ridge Hill mall is a well-known development by Forest City Enterprises.

Trump spent a year with Forest City, proving herself and learning the ropes of real estate. With some experience under her belt, she finally felt ready to follow her dream. It was time to join the family business.

Coming Home

In 2005 Trump returned to Trump Tower, this time to work in the Trump Organization. She finally felt ready to earn her keep. Her time at Forest City had given her something more to offer than just the family name. She had real-world experience, and she was eager to apply it to the family business.

While Trump was ready to work with her father, it was important to her that she stand on her own two feet. She got her own apartment, which she paid for herself. She knew that her family name had taken her a long way, but she didn't want to rely just on that.

"There's no denying that my family name, first-class education, and top-tier contacts gave me a bit of a leg up [on other college graduates]," Trump later wrote. "But I'm also a firm believer in making your own luck and making the most of your opportunities."

At first, Trump focused on the business. She excelled at negotiating deals. She quickly rose through the ranks at the Trump Organization, eventually earning a position as executive vice president of acquisitions and development.

Meanwhile, much of Donald Trump's attention had been focused on a different project—his television reality show, *The Apprentice*. The show, which had started in 2004, focused on a group of people who compete to earn a job under Trump. In 2006 Ivanka Trump joined her father on the show as one of his boardroom assistants. She replaced Carolyn Kepcher, an executive who had spent more than sixty episodes of the show by Donald Trump's side. In an interview, Donald Trump explained that his twenty-four-year-old daughter would help the show better appeal to a younger audience.

The Apprentice

The Apprentice premiered in January 2004 and became an instant hit. At the end of every show, Donald Trump narrowed down the field of candidates with his catchphrase, "You're fired!" Ivanka Trump joined the show in 2006 as a replacement for Carolyn Kepcher and then stayed on in 2007.

In 2007 the show evolved into *The Celebrity Apprentice* (with a brief return of *The Apprentice* in 2010). Celebrities competed for the title of Best Business Brain, with winnings being donated to charity. In 2017 the show became *The New Celebrity Apprentice*, hosted by movie star and former California governor Arnold Schwarzenegger, who opted not to return after one season as host.

Donald Trump arrives at a press tour sponsored by NBC, the network that aired *The Apprentice*.

Trump's role on *The Apprentice* came with both positives and negatives for her. Appearing on the show gave her a chance to show the world that she was a serious businesswoman. It helped her to establish a personal brand, which she would use to her advantage later. But joining her father also opened the door for criticism. Jay Leno of the *Tonight Show* joked, "That's good business sense. . . . Fire the competent people. Replace them with your children."

Donald and Ivanka Trump attend an NBC publicity event.

Trump took the criticism in stride. And she quickly carved out a space for herself on the program. She had her father's business sense, but she also had a softer side to which audiences could relate. Her business career was well established. With the show's booming popularity, her celebrity status was growing as well. Her name began showing up with increasing frequency in everything from newspapers to entertainment magazines and websites.

Trump wasn't content to bask in her newfound celebrity, however. In 2007 she started her own line of jewelry (soon followed by a clothing line). In September 2007, she opened her first jewelry boutique in New York. She remembered sitting in high-end jewelry stores with her mother and finding them terribly uncomfortable. So she designed her stores to be warm and inviting. She felt that shopping for jewelry should be fun, and she wanted her stores to give customers that experience.

Ivanka Trump at the launch of her jewelry line

Trump's marketing skill—especially her use of social media—helped make the lines a hit.

Trump was enjoying more and more success, and her businesses were helping to establish her own name and brand, beyond being the daughter of Donald Trump. Two years later, she published her first book. *The Trump Card: Playing to Win in Work and Life* featured her thoughts on business, the role of women in the workplace, and how her upbringing had influenced her.

Copies of *The Trump Card* greeted visitors at a party held at Trump Tower to celebrate the book.

Meanwhile, Trump was taking an interest in politics. Although she didn't identify herself with either political party, her support went largely to Democratic candidates. Among her political donations in 2007 was $1,000 to the presidential campaign of Hillary Clinton.

Starting a Family

Starting in 2005, Trump was in an on-and-off relationship with real estate developer Jared Kushner. The two had been set up for a lunch to talk about business and ended up hitting it off on a personal level. But as the couple grew more serious, a problem emerged. Kushner came from a devoutly Jewish family. His parents wanted him to marry a Jewish woman. Trump had been raised as a Christian.

Jared Kushner arrives at a movie premiere in New York.

The issue of religion almost drove the pair apart—until Trump decided on a solution. She agreed to convert to Judaism. She started the difficult and rigorous process of learning Jewish religious texts and laws. She worked for more than a year to convert. Once the process was finally complete, she took on a Hebrew name, Yael—although she still primarily went by her given name in daily life. She also adopted Jewish traditions such as eating a kosher diet (eating only foods sanctioned by Jewish law).

With that obstacle removed, the couple married on October 25, 2009. The Jewish ceremony was held at Trump National Golf Club in Bedminster, New Jersey. Guests at the wedding included celebrities such as former New York City mayor Rudy Giuliani, actors Russell Crowe and Natalie Portman, and journalist Barbara Walters. Trump wore a custom-made Vera Wang gown, along with diamond jewelry from her own collection.

Kushner and Trump smile for the camera at their 2009 wedding.

Jared Kushner

Ivanka Trump's husband, Jared Kushner, has become an instrumental part of the Trump family and campaign. He was born in 1981 into a wealthy New Jersey family. Kushner attended Harvard and New York University before following his father into the real estate industry. At the age of twenty-five, Kushner bought the *New York Observer* newspaper.

Kushner had been a longtime supporter of the Democratic Party. Yet he took on a key role in his father-in-law's presidential campaign, serving at first as a speechwriter and adviser. When Donald Trump fired his campaign manager in June 2016, Kushner took on many of the position's duties. He also served as a key member of Trump's transition team, preparing for the president-elect's entry into the White House. And as Trump prepared to assume the office of president, he named Kushner a senior White House adviser.

Some journalists and other observers worried that Kushner may not be objective in his role as adviser. They were concerned about his close personal ties to the Trumps. Yet Donald Trump thought Kushner was best suited for the job. As a result of Kushner's role and the trust the president places in him, Kushner seems poised to serve as an influential White House strategist.

Donald Trump shakes hands with Kushner at a campaign event.

Trump explained in a 2009 interview with *New York* magazine that their shared drive to succeed made the pair a good match. "Jared and I are very similar in that we're very ambitious," she said. "That's what makes it so amazing to be in a relationship with someone who is supportive of that."

The couple didn't wait long to start a family. On July 17, 2011, Trump gave birth to a daughter, Arabella Rose. In 2013, a son, Joseph Frederick, was born. He was followed by Theodore James three years later. Friends of the family describe Trump as a loving and devoted mother. She says she enjoys gardening with the children as well as cooking for her family. Juggling her career and family proved challenging, however. "Being a mother is the most rewarding experience, but also the most wild and stressful," Trump said in a 2016 interview.

Ivanka Trump holds daugher Arabella Rose at the Trump Invitational Grand Prix.

Both Trump and Kushner continued to work. That meant that during the workweek, they often didn't see their kids as much as they would have liked. However, they agreed to set aside weekends just for family time. The couple almost never made weekend plans. They would instead stay at home and turn off their mobile phones and other electronics to observe the Sabbath and to spend time with their children.

The Campaign Trail

Trump was taking on more and more responsibility with the family business. By 2015 it had become clear that her father planned to shift much of his role in the organization over to her. Her work ethic and attention to detail were a big part of the reason why. Another part was that her father's attention had increasingly begun splitting away from business and into politics.

Over the decades, Donald Trump had supported both Democrats and Republicans. But as the 2016 election season ramped up, he started aligning much more closely with the Republican Party. He also began winning more favor among some in the party. He was ready to capitalize on that growing popularity by running for the highest office in the United States—the presidency. Trump made his campaign official in July 2015. Ivanka Trump introduced him before he publicly announced his candidacy.

Donald Trump announces his candidacy for US president for the Republican Party.

At first, political experts largely dismissed the move. The list of Republican candidates was long and filled with seasoned politicians. Yet Trump was determined, and he slowly began to build momentum.

Ivanka Trump wasn't formally part of the campaign. Yet both she and Kushner were by her father's side for much of it—even though she was carrying her third child during the early stages of the race. Although she had previously supported Democrats, she became her dad's biggest ally. She traveled with the campaign, did interviews, and tried to appeal to younger voters and women.

Donald Trump didn't shy away from controversy during

the campaign. His words were often met with anger and hurt feelings. Some of the things he said put Ivanka Trump into awkward positions—including some comments that were demeaning toward women. She never spoke out directly against her father. Still, she made it clear that she didn't always agree with him.

"People ask me, do I ever disagree with my father?" she said. "It would be a little strange if I didn't."

To the surprise of many, Donald Trump's campaign didn't fade away. In February 2016, he began winning state contests that decide which candidate will represent each party in the national election. Trump lost the first state, Iowa. But then he went on a run, winning state after state. The biggest day of this phase of the presidential campaign is called Super Tuesday. It's when eleven states choose their candidates. Trump seized control of the Republican race for good, winning seven states. His campaign never looked back. By the time Ivanka Trump gave birth to her third baby, a son, in March, it was clear that her father would be the Republican candidate.

In July 2016—a year after Donald Trump made his candidacy official—Ivanka Trump traveled to Cleveland, Ohio, for the Republican National Convention. There, 2,472 delegates formally nominated Donald Trump as the party's candidate. As she had a year before, Ivanka Trump introduced her father. She gave a stirring speech that managed to promote her father without promoting his politics. Many called that moment the highlight of the convention—even over Donald Trump's acceptance speech.

The Trump campaign still had a hill to climb, though. The Democratic nominee, Hillary Clinton, had a big lead in most polls. In a strange twist of fate, one of Ivanka Trump's close friends was Chelsea Clinton. The daughters of the two candidates agreed to stay apart until after the election but promised that their friendship would remain regardless of the winner.

Chelsea Clinton *(right)* and Ivanka Trump vowed to stay friends even as their parents vied for the US presidency.

As the months dragged on, the campaign grew more and more combative. The candidates hurled insults at each other in a series of tense debates. They refused to even shake hands. The polling numbers tightened as election night approached, but Clinton held a lead.

Finally, Election Day arrived. Ivanka Trump brought five-year-old Arabella with her as she cast her vote for her father. Polling numbers still suggested that Clinton would win the election. But that's not what happened.

Donald Trump watches as Ivanka Trump places an I Voted sticker on daughter Arabella's jacket.

For reasons that experts struggled to explain, the election results didn't mirror the polling numbers. And by the early hours of November 9, it was clear. In what most considered a major surprise, Donald Trump had won the election. He would become the next president of the United States. Ivanka Trump was by his side, applauding, as he gave his acceptance speech.

First Daughter

Donald Trump got to work preparing for his presidency. He had two months to get ready before he took over for Barack Obama in January. One of the first questions that many asked was what his daughter's role in the White House would be.

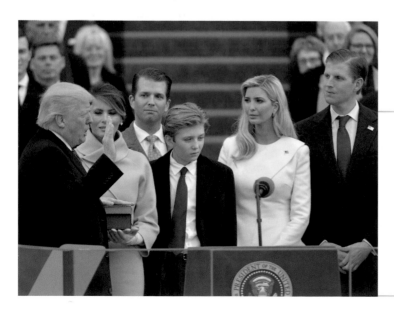

Donald Trump's family accompanies him as he is sworn in as US president in January 2017.

Ivanka Trump remained attentive to her father's political career after he was elected president.

In December the president-elect seemed to indicate that his daughter would be part of his White House in some way and that her brothers would run the Trump Organization in their absence. Indeed, later that month, Ivanka Trump and Kushner bought a home in Washington, DC, and joined a local synagogue. Many expected that Ivanka Trump would take on some of the traditional roles of a first lady, helping to drive and promote policy. However, in a 2017 interview, she said that she has no plans to fill such a role. She has stated that Donald's wife, Melania, will be the only first lady— although Melania planned to stay in New York while her and Donald's young son, Barron, finished school.

Donald, Barron, Melania, and Ivanka Trump stand before a crowd at a political event celebrating Donald Trump.

Being the daughter of the president and potentially working in the White House could pose unique problems for Ivanka Trump. Federal ethics laws restrict White House staff from operating businesses that could profit from their positions. Because of this, Trump was forced in January 2017 to step away from her role in the Trump Organization as well as temporarily give up control of her own businesses. For a woman who has worked her whole adult life to build those businesses, it's a big sacrifice.

"It's emotional," Trump explained. "I'm stepping away from my business. . . . My father will be president, and hopefully, I can be there to support him and to support those causes I've cared about my whole professional career."

Donald Trump's presidency could also have a wider-reaching impact on his daughter's businesses. The president remains a controversial figure, drawing scorn from his political opponents. Many experts believe that political backlash against the Trump presidency could seriously damage Ivanka Trump's brand. For example, some consumers have organized boycotts of products branded with her name due to concerns over her father's policies.

There is a trade-off for Trump, however. Her role in the White House will give her a chance to help drive policies about which she is passionate, including childcare reform. Trump didn't wait long. In January, even before her father was sworn into office, she helped present a childcare reform bill to key members of Congress. It's an issue that has traditionally had weak support among Republicans—a fact Trump will work to change.

Ever since she was a little girl sitting in her father's office, Ivanka Trump has wanted to follow in his footsteps, all while remaining her own person. How far would she be willing to follow? When she spoke at the 2016 Republican National Convention, some were already calling for an Ivanka Trump presidential run in 2024. During the campaign, she was asked if it was possible.

"It's not something I've ever been inclined to do," she said. "But I'm 34, so who knows? At this point I would never even contemplate it, but that doesn't mean that when I'm 50 I won't have a change of heart."

IMPORTANT DATES

1981 Ivanka Trump is born on October 30 in Manhattan, New York.

1989 Ivanka's life is turned upside down when her father gets involved in a public affair with Marla Maples.

1997 Trump appears on the cover of the May 1997 edition of *Seventeen* magazine. In August she serves as cohost of the Miss Teen USA pageant.

2000 Trump enrolls at Georgetown University.

2002 Trump enrolls at the Wharton School at the University of Pennsylvania, where she majors in finance and real estate.

2003 The documentary *Born Rich* is released. It features Trump and other young adults who were born into great wealth.

2004 Trump graduates from Wharton. She accepts a job at Forest City Enterprises.

2005 Trump leaves Forest City Enterprises and starts working for the Trump Organization.

2006 Trump appears on the TV show *The Apprentice* and goes on to become a regular on the show.

2009 Trump converts to Judaism and marries Jared Kushner. She publishes a book, *The Trump Card: Playing to Win in Work and Life*.

2015 Trump introduces her father when he announces his presidential candidacy.

2016 Trump introduces her father at the Republican National Convention as the party's presidential nominee. He goes on to win the presidency.

SOURCE NOTES

7 Paul Owen and Scott Bixby, "'The Greatest Asset Trump Has': Ivanka Gets Rave Reviews for Cleveland Speech," *Guardian* (US ed.), July 22, 2016, https://www.theguardian.com/us-news/2016/jul/22/ivanka-trump-republican-national-convention-speech.

8 Sunlen Serfaty and Theodore Schleifer, "Ivanka Trump Delivers in Prime-Time," *CNN*, July 22, 2016, http://www.cnn.com/2016/07/21/politics/ivanka-trump-republican-convention-speech.

9–10 Will Drabold, "Read Ivanka Trump's Speech at the Republican Convention," *Time*, July 21, 2016, http://time.com/4417579/republican-convention-ivanka-trump-transcript/.

10 Owen and Bixby, "Greatest Asset."

10 Ibid.

12 George Gurley, "Trump Power: Ivanka Trump," *Marie Claire*, January 29, 2007, http://www.marieclaire.com/career-advice/tips/a105/ivanka-trump/.

13 Ibid.

16 Jennifer Steinhauer, "Her Cheekbones (High) or Her Name (Trump)?," *New York Times*, August 17, 1997, http://www.nytimes.com/1997/08/17/style/her-cheekbones-high-or-her-name-trump.html.

17 Ibid.

19 Helen Pow, "'Born Rich' . . . and Now Richer: A Decade after Johnson & Johnson Heir Lifted the Lid on Growing Up with Millions for an HBO Documentary That Got Him Sued, MailOnline Looks at What the Film's Precocious Stars Are Doing Now," *Daily Mail.com*, October 22, 2013, http://www.dailymail.co.uk/news/article-2451031/Jamie-Johnson-documentary-A

-decade-Johnson--Johnson-heir-lifted-lid-growing-millions
-HBO-documentary-got-sued-MailOnline-looks-films-precocious
-stars-doing-now.html.

22 Ruth La Ferla, "Introducing the Ivanka," *New York Times*,
December 27, 2007, http://www.nytimes.com/2007/12/27
/fashion/27IVANKA.html.

24 Ivanka Trump, *The Trump Card: Playing to Win in Work and
Life* (New York: Simon & Schuster, 2009), PDF e-book.

26 "'Apprentice' Co-star Says Donald Didn't Dump Her," *ABC News*,
September 6, 2006, http://abcnews.go.com/GMA
/story?id=2399555.

32 Gabriel Sherman, "The Legacy," *New York*, July 12, 2009, http://
nymag.com/news/features/57891/.

32 Charlotte Triggs, "Inside Ivanka Trump's Chaotic Life Raising
Three Children with Husband Jared Kushner: 'I'm Exhausted
90 Percent of the Time,'" *People*, July 21, 2016, http://
celebritybabies.people.com/2016/07/21/ivanka-trump-raising
-three-children-jared-kushner-exhausted/.

35 Tim Teeman, "Ivanka Trump Talks Being a Mogul, a Mother, and
More," *Town & Country*, October 19, 2016, http://www
.townandcountrymag.com/society/money-and-power/a4616
/ivanka-trump-2016/.

40–41 Lauren Effron and John Santucci, "Ivanka Trump Says She Will
Not Be Filling In as First Lady in Trump Administration," *ABC
News*, January 19, 2017, http://abcnews.go.com/Politics/ivanka
-trump-filling-lady-trump-administration/story?id=44871559.

41 Teeman, "Ivanka Trump."

SELECTED BIBLIOGRAPHY

Steinhauer, Jennifer. "Her Cheekbones (High) or Her Name (Trump)?" *New York Times*, August 17, 1997. http://www.nytimes .com/1997/08/17/style/her-cheekbones-high-or-her-name-trump.html.

Teeman, Tim. "Ivanka Trump Talks Being a Mogul, a Mother, and More." *Town & Country*, October 19, 2016. http://www.townandcountrymag .com/society/money-and-power/a4616/ivanka-trump-2016/.

Trump, Donald. *Trump: The Art of the Deal.* New York: Ballantine Books, 1987.

Trump, Ivanka. *The Trump Card: Playing to Win in Work and Life.* New York: Simon & Schuster, 2009. PDF e-book.

Widdicombe, Lizzie. "Ivanka and Jared's Power Play: How the Patrician Couple Came to Have an Outsized Influence on a Populist Presidential Campaign." *New Yorker*, August 22, 2016. http://www .newyorker.com/magazine/2016/08/22/ivanka-trump-and-jared -kushners-power-play.

FURTHER READING

BOOKS

Baum, Margaux. *Fashion and Clothing.* New York: Rosen, 2017. Ivanka Trump has made a name for herself in the fashion industry. Learn more about this industry, as well as about fashion and clothing in general, in this fun read.

McAuliffe, Bill. *The U.S. Presidency.* Mankato, MN: Creative Education, 2016. Check out this title for information on the office that Ivanka Trump's father rose to in January 2017.

Sherman, Jill. *Donald Trump: Outspoken Personality and President.* Minneapolis: Lerner Publications, 2017. Read about the background and political success of Ivanka Trump's father, US president Donald Trump.

WEBSITES

Ivanka Trump
http://ivankatrump.com
Ivanka Trump's official website includes a biography of her as well as information on style, travel, her favorite words of wisdom, and more.

The Wharton School
https://www.wharton.upenn.edu
Do you dream of succeeding in business like Ivanka Trump? Then you may be interested in this website about the United States' first business school, which she attended.

The White House
https://www.whitehouse.gov
Learn more about the Trump administration and the office of the US president.

INDEX